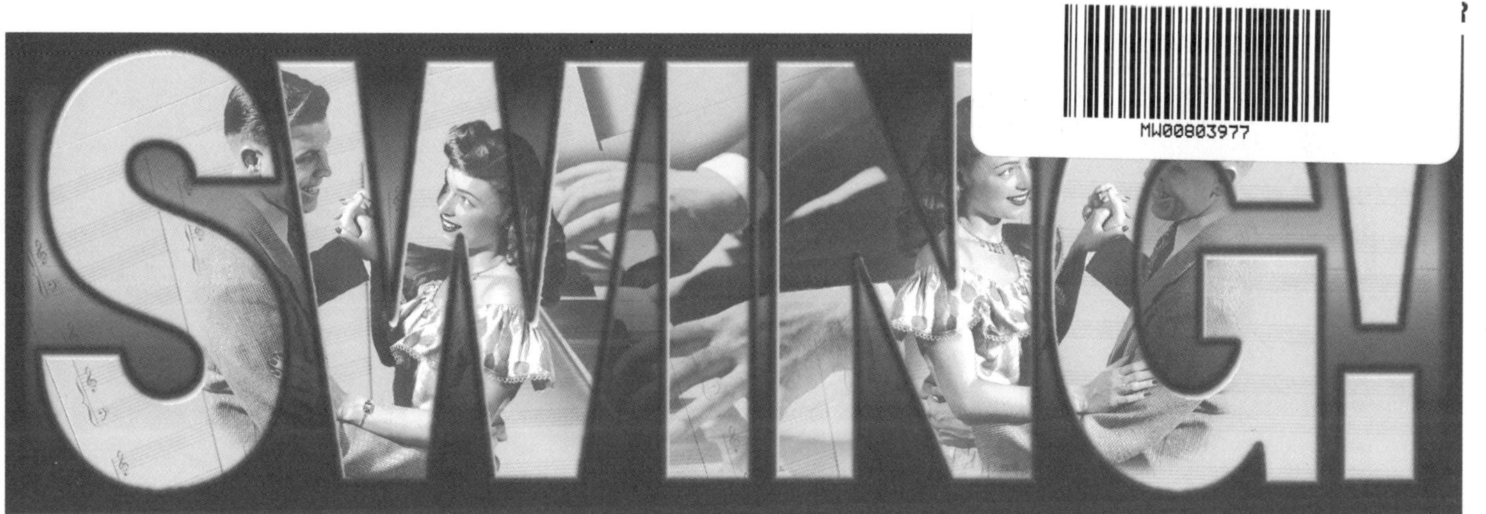

THE ULTIMATE COLLECTION

Project Manager: Tony Esposito
Cover Design: Martha Lucia Ramirez

CONTENTS

Recorded by GLENN MILLER

ALONG THE SANTA FE TRAIL

Words by
AL DUBIN & EDWINA COOLIDGE

Music by
WILL GROSZ

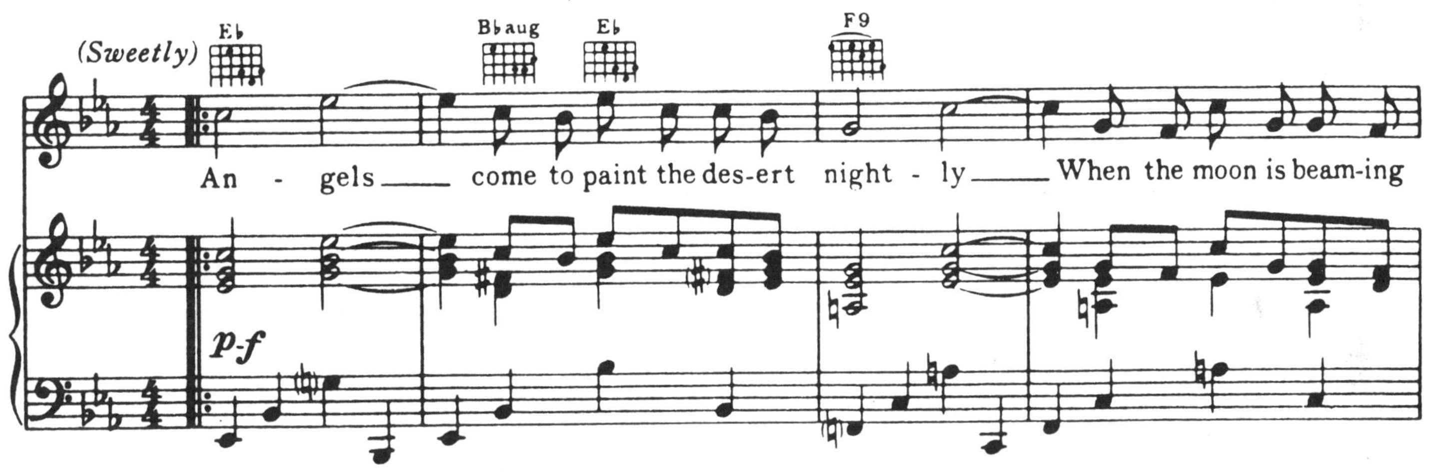

Eb
Bbaug
Eb
Bbaug
F9
Star - dust scat-tered all a-long the high - way
Ab6
Abm6
Ab6
On a rain-bow col-ored sky - way A-LONG THE SAN-TA FE
Eb
Bbm7
Eb7
Ab
TRAIL. Be - side you I'm rid - ing
Abm6
Eb
ev-'ry hill and dale while shad - ows hide you

F7
Abm6
Bbaug
just like a pret-ty pur-ple veil; There-by hangs a tale, I
Eb
Bbaug
Eb
Bbaug
F9
found you and the moun-tains that sur-round you
Ab6
Abm6
Ab6
are the walls I built a-round you A-LONG THE SAN-TA FE
1. Eb
Abmaj7
Bb9
2. Eb
TRAIL.
TRAIL.

Recorded by TEX BENECKE & THE GLENN MILLER ORCHESTRA

A GAL IN CALICO

Words by
LEO ROBIN

Music by
ARTHUR SCHWARTZ

E♭ E♭maj7 E♭6 E♭maj7 Fm7 B♭9 B♭7(♭9)

Work - in' with a ro - de - o, go from town to town.
Gon - na quit the ro - de - o, gon - na set - tle down,

E♭ E♭maj7 E♭6 E♭maj7 Fm7 B♭9

See most ev - 'ry kind - a gal, ev - 'ry kind - a gown. But
buy a bolt of cal - i - co for a wed - din' gown. Then,

E♭ B♭m7 E♭7 A♭maj7 Fm7 G7 C7 F9(♭5) B♭7

who made my heart sing? Yip - pee yi! Yip - pee yo! My
will I fence her in.

E♭ Cm7 Fm7 B♭9 E♭ Fm7 B♭7 E♭

lit - tle gal in cal - i - co.

pp

Recorded by LARRY ELGART

ZING! WENT THE STRINGS OF MY HEART

Words and Music by
JAMES F. HANLEY

Eb 3fr. Cm Eb F7 Bb Ebm6 Bb°7 Bb7 Eb
Zing! went the strings of my heart. 'Twas like a
Eb Cm 3fr. G7 Cm 3fr. Fm C7 Fm Bb7
breath of Spring, I heard a rob-in sing A-bout a nest set a-part,
C9 B9 Bb9 C9 B9 Bb9 Ab 4fr. Eb Ab 4fr. Abm 4fr.
All na-ture seemed to be
mf

Eb
Abm
4fr.
In per-fect har-mo-ny,
Eb
3fr.
Cm
Eb
F7
Bb7
Bb7+5
Eb
Abm6
Zing! went the strings of my heart.
Fm7
Bb7
mp
Your eyes made skies seem blue a-gain,
What else could I do a-gain, But
Am7-5
D7
F7
keep re-peat-ing through a-gain "I love you, love you!"
Bb9
mf
poco rit.
mf espr. e poco rit.
p a tempo

Eb
Bb7
Cm
3fr.
G7
Fm
C7
p a tempo
I still re-call the thrill, I guess I al-ways will, I hope 'twill
mf
C9
B9
Bb9
Ab
4fr.
nev-er de-part,
Dear, with your
Abm
lips to mine
A rhap-so-dy di-vine.
Zing! went the
F7
Bb7+5
Fm7
1
2
strings of my heart.
heart.
f
8va bassa

A-TISKET, A-TASKET

Words and Music by
ELLA FITZGERALD and
VAN ALEXANDER

Fm7 Bb7 Fm7 Bb7 Fm7 Bb7 Eb Eb7
lit - tle girl - ie picked it up And took it to the mar - ket, She was
Ab Abm6 Eb Ebmaj7 Eb7 Eb7+
truck - in' on down the Av - e - nue without a sin - gle thing to do; She was
Ab Ab+ Abm6 Eb Cm7 F7 F7b5 Bb7 Bb7+
peck, peck, peck - in' all a - round. When she spied it on the ground A -
Eb Ab Eb Bb7 Eb Ab Eb Edim
tis - ket, a - tas - ket She took my yel - low bas - ket And

Fm7
Bb7
Fm7
Bb7
1.
Eb
if she does-n't bring it back, I think that I shall die.
Ab
Eb
Ab
Bb7+
2.
Eb
A - die.
(Was it red?)
Ab6
Eb
Ab6
Eb
No, No, No, No,
(Was it brown?)
No, No, No, No,
(Was it blue?)
Ab6
Eb
Ab6
B♮7
Bb7
Eb
No, No, No, No, Just a lit-tle yel - low bas - ket.

From the M-G-M Musical Production "CABIN IN THE SKY"

TAKING A CHANCE ON LOVE

Words by JOHN LATOUCHE
and TED FETTER

Music by
VERNON DUKE

Cmaj 7
Edim
Dm7
G7
C
C+
Chorus, Moderately
Here I go a - gain I hear those trum-pets blow a - gain
Here I come a - gain I'm gon - na make things hum a - gain
Here I slip a - gain a - bout to take that tip a - gain
mp
Am
Am7
D7
Dm7
G7
Em7
Cm
Dm7
G7
all a - glow a - gain Tak - ing A Chance On Love
act - ing dumb a - gain Tak - ing A Chance On Love
got my grip a - gain Tak - ing A Chance On Love
Cmaj 7
Edim
Dm7
G7
C
C+
Here I slide a - gain a - bout to take that ride a - gain
Here I stand a - gain a - bout to beat the band a - gain
Now I prove a - gain that I can make life move a - gain
Am
Am7
D7
Dm7
G7
C
star - ry - eyed a - gain Tak - ing A Chance On Love. I
feel - ing grand a - gain Tak - ing A Chance On Love. I
in the groove a - gain Tak - ing A Chance On Love I

Gm7 C7 F Cdim Gm7 Gdim F
thought that cards — were a frame - up — I nev - er — would try But
nev - er dreamed in my slum - bers — and bets were — ta - boo But
walk a - round — with a horse - shoe — in clo - ver — I lie And
mf
Fm7 B♭7 E♭ Gdim Fm7 A♭7 G7+
now I'm tak - ing the game up — and the ace of hearts is high
now I'm play - ing the num - bers on a lit - tle dream for two
broth - er rab - bit of course you — bet - ter kiss your foot good - bye
C Edim Dm7 G7 C C+
Things are mend - ing now — I see a rain - bow blend - ing now —
Wad - ing in a - gain — I'm lead - in' with my chin a - gain —
On the ball a - gain — I'm rid - in' for a fall a - gain —
sf mp
Am Am7 D7 Dm7 G7 C Dm7 G7 C
1. 2.
we'll have our hap - py end - ing now Tak - ing A Chance On Love.
I'm start - in' out to win a - gain Tak - ing A Chance On Love.
I'm gon - na give my all a - gain Tak - ing A Chance On Love.
f
3
sfz

AND THE ANGELS SING

Words by
JOHNNY MERCER

Music by
ZIGGIE ELMAN

F7-5 Bb7 Eb Bbm7 Eb7 Bbm7 Eb7 Ebdim Eb
Sud-den-ly the set-ting is strange, I can see wa-ter and
Bbm7 Eb7 Bbm7 Eb7 Bbm7 Eb7 Eb7 Bbm7
moon-light beam-ing, sil-ver waves that break on some un-dis-cov-ered shore;
Eb7 Bbm7 Eb7 Bbm7 Eb7 Ebdim Eb
then sud-den-ly I see it all change, long win-ter nights with the
Bbm7 Eb7 Bbm7 Eb7 Ab6 C7 Fm F7 F7-5 Bb7 Eb Cm7 Fm7 Bb7-9
can-dles gleam-ing, thru it all your face that I a - dore. You

Eb
Cm7
Fm7
Bb7
Fm7
Eb
Eb6
Bdim
Cm
smile, And The An-gels Sing And 'tho its
Fm
Edim
Fm7
Bb
F7
B7
Bb7
Eb
Cm7
Fm7
Bb7-9
Eb
just a gen-tle mur-mur at the start, We kiss,
Fm7
Bb7
Fm7
G7
Gdim
F7
Fm
Bbdim
Fm
C7
And The An-gels Sing and leave their mu-sic ring-ing
1.
2.
Abm6
Db7
Eb
Cm7
Fm7
Bb7-9
Eb
Ab
Eb
in my heart. We heart.
f
ff
rit.

TUXEDO JUNCTION

Words by
BUDDY FEYNE

Music by
ERSKINE HAWKINS, WILLIAM JOHNSON
and JULIAN DASH

Medium swing

Bb Eb F7 Bb Eb F7

Feel-in' low, Rock-in' slow,

mf

Bb Eb Edim Bb F7 Bb

Want to go, Right back where I be - long.

Chorus

F7 Bb Eb9 F7 Bb

Way down South, in Bir - ming-ham, I mean South in Al -
drive or walk for miles to get jive that South-

mf

Eb9 F7 Bb Eb9 Edim

- a - bam's an old place where peo - ple go to dance
- ern style, S - low jive that makes you want to dance

Bb F7 1. Bb F7 2. Bb Bb9

the night a - way. They all
'til break of day. It's a

Eb6
Eb7
Bb6
junc - tion where the town folks meet.
Eb7
Bb9
Eb6
Eb7
At each func - tion, in their
Bb6
Gm7
Cm7
F7
Bb
Eb9
F7
tux they greet you. Come on down, for - get your care. Come on
Bb
Eb9
F7
Bb
down, You'll find me there. So long town! I'm head -
Eb9
Edim
Bb
F7
Bb
- in' for Tux - e - do Junc - tion now.

Recorded by COUNT BASIE

UNTIL I MET YOU

(Corner Pocket)

Words and Music by
DON WOLF and FREDDY GREENE

APRIL IN PARIS

Lyrics by
E.Y. HARBURG

Music by
VERNON DUKE

E7+5 E7 Gm6 A7 Fmaj7 F°7 C6 F°7 Fm6
mf
prise. I nev-er knew the charm of Spring, Nev-er met it face to
C Bm7-5 E7-9 Am F♯m7-5 B7+5 B7
face. I nev-er knew my heart could sing, Nev-er missed a warm em-
Emaj7 E6 Gsus4 G7 Fm B C C6 Em7-5 C+ A7+5
brace, till A-pril in Par-is, Whom can I run to
D7 G♯m6 Am6 D9 G7sus4 G7 1. C G7/6 G9 2. C F C
What have you done to my heart? heart?

TRAV'LIN' LIGHT

Words by
JOHNNY MERCER

Music by
JIMMY MUNDY and TRUMMY YOUNG

Gm7
C7
Gm7
Gb
F
Gb9
F9
Bb9
Bb
I'm TRAV-'LIN' LIGHT
No one to see
Am
F
B9
F
Bb9
Am7
Ab7
I'm free as the breeze
No one but me
Gm7
C9
F
Fdim
Gm7
and my memories
Some luck-y night
C9
F9
Cdim
F
Fdim
Gm7
he may come back a-gain
but un-til then
Gm7
C7
Gm
1
Gb
F
Fdim
Gm
2
Gb
F
I'm TRAV-'LIN' LIGHT.
I'm TRAV-'LIN' LIGHT.

AVENUE "C"

Words by
JON HENDRICKS and DAVE LAMBERT

Music by
BUCK CLAYTON

D
A7sus
most of the hard-to-for-get streets. It's
real-ly and tru-ly the dil-ly of all of my pet streets, hey, hey, hey, ev-'ry-bod-y now,
D
G7
D
D7
come go walk-in' with me; now walk up Av-en-ue "C". Now, chicks-
G7
D7
all look-in' so pret - ty, they don't gim-me no pit -

F♯m7
B7
Em7
A7-9
y. Av - en - ue "C" is the groov - i - est in the
D
Em7 (A bass)
G7
cit - y. I nev-er dug an Av-en - ue more en-joy-a-ble to
D
Am7
A♭7(♯9)
Gm7
C7sus
me; "C" Av-en - ue is groov - y, yes, it was
D7 (F♯ bass)
F9(♯11)
Em7 (A bass)
A7
groov-y as it could be. Walk with me down Av-en-ue "C",

D7
A7sus
D
(A bass)
G
man, I real-ly hope to say "come on, ba - by," while we
D7
G9
D
ram - ble. Walk be - side me while we ram - ble,
F♯m7
F7
Em7
A7sus
you dig it too; I feel you do. What a scen - ic hike,
D (F♯ bass)
G (F bass)
Em7
F♯m (D♯ bass)
D13
E♭13
it's a walk that you're bound to like. You got "B" on the one side, "D"

E13
Fm7
B♭7
on the oth - er, "C" in the mid - dle; ba - by, the
E♭7
A♭7
E♭7
rea-son that you're feel-in' so down babe, is 'cause you live in Stuy - ve - sant
E♭7
A♭7
Town, babe. I dug you down in Ham - il - ton Fish, babe, and
E♭7
F♯dim
Fm7
re - al - ized that you were my dish, babe. Walk - in' home and you can walk

Bb7sus
(G bass)
Eb
Gb7
Fm7
Bb7
Eb
with me; walk - in' hand in hand on Av - en - ue "C", oh babe, and
Ab7
Eb
while we're walk-in', we can do some talk - in', while the peo - ple dig us, won-d'ring
Ab7
Eb (G bass)
what we're put - tin' down. While we, hap - py as we
Gbm
Fm7
Bb7(#9)
can be, glide on, tak - ing life in stride up to Murph-

Eb(G bass)
Gbm
Fm7
y Park, there be - side the riv - er.
Well, our
D
G7
D7
feet got rhy - thm 'n' we walk with em. Well, our
Pure ped-al syn-co - pa - tion, de-mand-ing ad-mir - a - tion.
G7
D7
step is snap - py be-cause we're so
Dig, peo - ple step a - side now, we're tak - in' life in
A
A (G bass)
hap - py.)
stride now. Av-en - ue "C", your vi - bra-tions are fol -

(F# bass)
A
(F bass)
A
(A bass)
G
D
low - ing me,
oh
ev - 'ry - bod - y bus -
yes
yes
G7
D7
i - ly look - in',
me and ba - by's stead - i - ly cook - in'.
yes
yes
G7
D7
Start at one end,
talk - in' and mov - in',
to the oth - er, wig -
yes
yes
yes
yes
A7
A7sus
gin' and groov - in'.
You should,
I would,
you could,
So come
and view
this A - ven -

D7
G7
D
it's good "C" Av-en - ue, see it my way, no bet-ter
ue, walk on, talk - in',
G7
F♯m7
view on a high-way. Big town, you don't know til you see it, I nev-er saw
walk on.
F7
Em7
A7sus
3
such a won-der-ful sight. You're gon-na love it.
drum solo
I'm hip, When you dig it you'll
you'll

stop and lin - ger; what a pleas - ure and what a swing - er,
flip You'll pop your top;
D
D (F# bass)
G
G#dim
G (A bass)
D
go dig it, cop that view. It's bound to thrill you,
go,
come on, come on
go dig it, cop that view, it's bound to thrill you.
go go
come on, come on now.
1.
2.
Go; dig it, cop that view, it's bound to thrill you.
Go, go.

STOMPIN' AT THE SAVOY

Lyric by
ANDY RAZAF

Music by
BENNY GOODMAN, CHICK WEBB and
EDGAR SAMPSON

How my heart is sing-in' while the band is
swing-in' Nev-er tired of romp-in' and
stomp-in' with you, At the Sa-voy What joy, a per-fect hol-i-day
Sa-voy, where we can glide and sway Sa-voy,
there let me stomp a-way, with you.
mf
cresc.
mp

mf
cresc.
f

mf
cresc.
f
dim.
rit.
p

BEGIN THE BEGUINE

French Version by
EMELIA RENAUD
Spanish Version by
MARIA GREVER

Words and Music by
COLE PORTER

Bb
Bb6
Bb
Bbmaj7
Bb6
I'm with you once more under the stars And
Le ciel é - toi - lé luit pour tou - jours, La
Hoy so - los 'al fin, cer - ca del mar Cual
Bb
F7
down by the shore an or - ches - tra's play - ing, And e - ven the palms
vague en - chan - tée pro - té - ge notr' a - mour La bri - se ber - ce
sua - ve vai - ven lle - ga a mis o - i - dos El ru - mor de be -
Cm
F7
Eb
Cm
Cm7
F7
seem to be sway - ing When they be - gin the Be -
dou - ce - ment les fleurs, Quand tu me prends dans tes
- sos es - con - di - dos En la can - ción Tro - pi -
Bb
Bbm
Eb7
Ab
guine. To live it a - gain is past all en - deav - our,
bras. Je ne puis vi - vre ces mo - ments en - chan - teurs,
cal Vol - ver a vi - vir a - que - llos ins - tan - tes

Ex-cept when that tune clutch-es my heart, And
Quc lors-que j'en-tends bat-trc ton cœur, Quand
En que me ro-bas - - te el co-ra - zón En
cresc.
there we are, swear-ing to love for-ev - er, And prom-is-ing
nous sommes la ju-rant d'ai-mer sans ces - se, Et pro-met-tant
que ju - rè A - mar-te e-ter - na - men - te Con el fue-go ar-
mf più espr.
nev - er, nev - er to part. What mo-ments di-vine,
fi - dé - li - té tou - jours. Quels mo-ments di-vins,
dien - te de mi pa - sión Mo - men-to fe - liz,
dim.
p
what rap-ture se-rene, Till clouds came a-long to dis-perse the joys we had
quelle fé - li - ci - té, Quand une om - bre vient dis-per-ser les joies qui furent
di-vi-no e i-de - al Has - ta que la llu-via lle - gó pa-ra dis-per-

tast - ed And now when I hear peo-ple curse the chance that was wast - ed,
nô - tres Nous fai-sant croire à un a - ve - nir triste et mo - ro - se
sar - nos Y con la mas cruél mal-di - ción qui - so con-de - nar - nos
I know but too well what they mean; So don't
Tout sem-ble per-du à ja - mais. Oui re -
A u - na so - le - dad sin i - gual Nun-ca ol -
mf più espr.
let them be - gin the Be - guine, Let the
prends moi en - core dans tes bras, Que notr'
vi - des tu rit - - - mo sen - sual Que la
love that was once a - fire re-main an em - ber; Let it
a - mour ar - dent laisse au moins u - ne flam - me, Qu'il reste
lla - ma de a-mor sin - ce - ro no se a - pa - ga Ni el de-

sleep like the dead de - sire I on - ly re - mem - ber When they be - gin
de notr' a - mour tou - jours un peu de cen - dres Quand tu me prends
se - o de a - mar por siem - pre nun - ca se a - ca - ba Con la can - ción
dim.
p
the Be - guine. Oh yes, let them be - gin the Be - guine, make them
dans tes bras. Lais - se moi me blot - tir à nou - veau dans tes
tro - pi - cal Can - ta siem - pre tu rit - mo, sen - sual, sin ce -
f molto espr.
play Till the stars that were there be - fore re - turn a -
bras, Pour que les é - toi - les re - vien - nent sur nos
sar Has - ta que las es - tre - llas vuel - van a a - lum -
bove you, Till you whis - per to me once more, "Dar - ling, I love you!"
tê - tes, Que je t'en - ten - de mur - mu - rer "Dar - ling" je t'ai - me,
brar - nos Y que un be - so fe - bril de a - mor vuel - va a jun - tar - nos
mf
dim.

And we sud-den-ly know what heav-en we're in,
Et nous re-trou-ve-rons no-tre pa-ra-dis,
En el dul-ce ru-mor del rit-mo sen-sual
When they be-gin the Be-guine,
Quand tu me prends dans tes bras.
De la can-ción tro-pi-cal
When they be-gin the Be-guine.
Quand tu me prends dans tes bras.
De la can-ción tro-pi-cal
ten.
rit.
a tempo
dim.
p
pp
8

OPUS ONE

Words and Music by
SY OLIVER and SID GARRIS

A9 Am7/D D7 G C7 G
that's the main thing, to make with the feet,- 'Cause ev-'ry-one is swing-in' to-day,- So,- I'll call it
Bb Gm7 Cm7 F7-9 Bb6 G7+5 C9 F7+5 Db Bbm7
O-PUS ONE! It's not for Sam-my Kaye,- Hey!- hey!- hey!- it's O-PUS ONE! It's
Ebm7 Ab7-9 Db6 G
got to swing, not sway. May - be, if Mis-ter Les Brown could
C7 A9
make it re-nown And Ray An-tho-ny could swing it for me,- There's nev-er a doubt you'll
Am7/D D9 G C7 1. G G#o7 Am7 D7 2. G Eb9 G6
knock your-self out,- When-ev-er you can hear O-PUS ONE. - I'm

BEI MIR BIST DU SCHÖN
(MEANS THAT YOU'RE GRAND)

Original Lyrics by
JACOB JACOBS
English Version by
SAMMY CAHN and SAUL CHAPLIN

Music by
SHOLOM SECUNDA

Dm
F7
heart grew light__ And this old world seemed__ new to
E7
Am
Dm6
E7
me, You're real-ly swell I have__ to ad-mit, you__ de-serve ex-
Am
Dm6
E7
Am
pres-sions that__ real-ly fit you,__ And so I've racked my brain,__hop-ing
Dm
F7
E7
to ex-plain__ all the things that you__ do to me;

REFRAIN

* Pronounced "By Meer Bist Doo Shane"

Am
Dm
Am
I could say "Bel - la, Bel - la," ev - en say "Voon-der - bar," Each lan-guage
Dm
F7
E
E dim.
E7
Am
on - ly helps me tell you how grand you are, I've tried to ex - plain,
F7
E7
"BEI MIR BIST DU SCHÖN," So, kiss me and say
F7
E7
1. Am
Dm
E7
2. Am
Dm
E7
Am
you un - der - stand. "BEI

BIG NOISE FROM WINNETKA

Words by
GIL RODIN and
BOB CROSBY

Music by
BOB HAGGART and
RAY BAUDUC

Fm6
Big Noise blew right out a - gain.
C7-9
Fm6
C7-9
Girls were sigh - ing, their boy friends
Fm6
C7-9
Fm6
C7
cry - ing, their hearts were break - ing when
D♭7
C7
Fm6
Big Noise blew in from Win - net

Fm6
ka,
Big Noise
blew right
out
a - gain.
Fm6
C7-9
Fm6
Stop,
look,
lis-ten,
Bbm6
C7
Bbm6
C7
lis-ten
to
the
Big
Noise.
Fm6
I'm called the
Big
Noise
from
Win-net
- ka;
mf

Fm6
and I play ro - man - tic parts.
Bbm6
C7+
C7
Fm6
I just blew in from Win-net
- ka
where I
broke a mil - lion hearts.
Bbm6
C7
Fm
Fm6
C7-9
Now I've had

Fm6
C7-9
Fm6
C7-9
my fun and yet, there's just one who got me
Fm6
C7
Db7
C7
Fm6
from the start.
Ex - it
Big Noise from Win-net - ka,
Fm6
en - ter Big Noise in your heart.
ff

PENNSYLVANIA 6-5000

Lyric by
CARL SIGMAN

Music by
JERRY GRAY

G
C9
Chorus, Moderately (with a swing)
Num-bers I've got by the doz - en
ev-'ry-one's un-cle and
p-mf
Ddim
Am7
D7
cous - in
But I can't live with-out buzz - in'
G
Guitar Tacet
(spoken)
D7+
Penn-syl-van-ia Six, Five Thou-sand
I've got a sweet-y I know there
Some-one who sets me a - glow there
Gives me the sweet-est "hel -
lo there"
Penn-syl-van-ia Six, Five Thou-sand
Am
B7+
B7
We don't say "how are

Em
Am
B7+
B7
Em
E7-5
— you" and ver - y sel - dom ask — "what's new?" — In-
A7 add6
A7
D
C7
B7
E9
A7
stead we start and end each call — with "ba - by con - fi - den - tial - ly I —
D7
Eb9
D7
G
C9
— love you" — may - be it sounds a bit fun - ny —
G
Ddim
Am7
D7
When I'm a - way from my hon - ey — here's what I do with my mon - ey —
1. G
Guitar Tacet
(spoken)
D+
2. G
Guitar Tacet
(spoken)
G6
Penn-syl-van-ia Six, Five Thou-sand
Penn-syl-van-ia Six, Five Thou-sand

BOB WHITE
(Whatcha Gonna Swing Tonight?)

Words by
JOHNNY MERCER

Music by
BERNIE HANIGHEN

F7
Fm7
Bb7
F7
Abm6
Bb7
Eb
Eb6
Eb dim.
Fm7
Bob White! What-cha gon-na swing to - night?
Eb
Cm7
Cm6
D7
Gm
C dim.
Gm
Gm7
E-ven the owl Tells me you're foul, Sing-in' those lul - la -
C9
Fm
G dim.
Fm
Gm
Bb7 +5
by notes, Don't be a bring-down, If you can swing down, Gim-me those high notes!

Eb
Fm7
Eb
Ab
Cm6
Cm
Ab7
There's a lot-ta talk a-bout you, Bob, And they're say-in' you're "off the cob,"
F7
Fm7
Bb7
C7-5
C7
Fm
Fm7
Fake it, Mis-ter B. Take it,
D7-5
D7
Eb
Eb6
Bb7
(Sing)
fol-low me, Bob White! (Whistle) We're gon-na break it up to-
p
1
Eb6
2
Eb6
night! I was talk-in' to the night!
R. H.

ON THE ATCHISON, TOPEKA AND THE SANTA FE

Lyric by
JOHNNY MERCER

Music by
HARRY WARREN

Moderately *(with rhythm)*

f *mf*

Moderately *(with rhythm)*

G7 C G7 C F

Do yuh hear that whis-tle down the line? I fig-ure that it's en-gine num-ber

mp

C F6 C G+ C G7 C G7 C Gdim Am A♭7

for-ty nine, She's the on-ly one that-'ll sound that way. On The

C G♯dim Am Dm7 G7 C G7

Atch-i-son, To-pe-ka And The San-ta Fe See the

C
G7
C
F
ol' smoke ris - in' 'round the bend,— I reck - on that she knows she's gon - na
C
F6
C
G+
C
G7
C
G7
C
G#dim
Am
Ab7
meet a friend,— Folks a - round these parts get the time o' day— From The
C
G#dim
Am
Dm7
G7
C
Eb7
Ab6
Atch - i - son, To - pe - ka And The San - ta Fe.— Here she comes! Ooh,—
Ebmaj7
Ab6
Ab
Ebmaj7
Ab6
Eb
— Ooh,— Ooh, Hey, Jim! yuh bet - ter git the rig!—
Ab6
Ebmaj7
Ab6
— Ooh, Ooh,— Ooh, She's

Cm Ebmaj7 Fm6 Cm7 Fm Abmaj7 Fm6 G7 C G7 C
got a list o' pas-sen-gers that's pret-ty big_ And they'll all want lifts to
Brown's Ho-tel,_ 'Cause lots o' them been trav-el-in' for quite a spell,_ All the
F C F6 C G+
C G7 Cmaj7 C7 F6 C G#dim Am Dm7
way from Phil-a-del-phi-ay,_ On The Atch-i-son, To-pe-ka And The
1 2
G7 C G7 G7 C
San-ta Fe._ Do yuh San-ta Fe._
G9 (addE)
(Single notes)
C D E G E D C A G
C B C Fdim Cdim C

BUGLE CALL RAG

By
JACK PETTIS, BILLY MEYERS
and ELMER SCHOEBEL

Cm7 F7 Bb Eb7 Bb Bb7 Gm Bb7
brag 'Bout that bu-gle call rag.
CHORUS
Eb7 Bb Dm7 Dm7b5 G7
Hold me ba - by, Let's syn - co - pate to that blue mel - o - dy, Just
mf
C7 F7 Bb Bb7 Gm Bb7
hes - i - tate while a break they take shh!
Eb7 Bb Dm7 Dm7b5 G7 C7
While we're danc-ing Please hold me tight, Step live - ly don't lag, Swing a-long
F7 1. Bb Eb7 Bb Bb7 Gm Bb7 2. Bb Eb7 Bb
to that bu-gle call rag. rag.
fz

ONE O'CLOCK JUMP

By COUNT BASIE

dim.
p
cresc.
mf
f

dim.
p
f
mf
8va
dim.

8va
p
8va
mf
8va
loco
p
mf

8va
f
8va
8va
8va
loco
p
cresc.
f
mf
p
accel.
pp

CHATTANOOGA CHOO CHOO

Lyrics by
MACK GORDON

Music by
HARRY WARREN

Dm7
G7
G9
C
I've got my fare
and just a tri-fle to spare.
C7
B♭(C sus)
C7
F
C7
F
Gm7
C7
F
C7
You leave the Penn-syl-va-nia sta-tion 'bout a quar-ter to four,
read a mag-a-zine and then you're
mf
F
F9
B♭
Fdim
F
D+
D7
G-9
in Bal-ti-more, Din-ner in the din-er, noth-ing could be fin-er than to have your ham'n eggs in
A♭m6
C9
F
C7
F
Gm7
C7
Car-o-li-na. When you hear the whis-tle blow-in' eight to the bar Then

F
C7
F
F9
B♭
Fdim
F
D+
D7
— you know that Ten-nes-see is not ver-y far, — Shov - el all the coal in, got - ta keep it roll-in'
G-9
C7
F
G7
C
Woo, Woo, Chat - ta-noo - ga there — you are. —
mp
C
Cdim
C6
There's gon-na be a cer-tain par-ty at the sta-tion Sat - in and lace, —
Dm7
G7
G9
C
— I used to call fun-ny face. —

Cdim
C6
C7
F
She's gon - na cry
un - til I tell her that I'll nev - er roam,
Ab7
D7-5
C
Am7
D7
Dm7
G-9
C
So Chat - ta - noo - ga Choo-Choo won't you choo-choo me home.
Cm6
C7
(A sus)
Cm6
C7
Am7
Chat - ta - noo - ga Choo-Choo won't
D7-5
Dm7
G-9
C
G7
C
C
(Single note)
you choo - choo me home.
sfz

MINNIE, THE MOOCHER

Words and Music by
CAB CALLOWAY and IRVING MILLS

Chorus
Em
Ho de ho de ho, (Ho de ho de ho) Rah de
Hi de hi de hi, (Hi de hi de hi) Ree de
dah de dah, (Rah de dah de dah) Tee - dle dee de dee (Tee - dle -
dah de doo, (Ree de dah de doo) Bo - de dah do dah (Bo - de -
1. B7 Em Am6 Em B7
dee de dee) Ho de ho de ho, (Ho de ho - o de ho)
dah do dah) Ho de
2. She
2. B7 Em B7 Em Am6 B7 Em
Ho de ho Poor Min, Poor Min, Poor Min.
fz

DO NOTHIN' TILL YOU HEAR FROM ME

Lyrics by
BOB RUSSELL

Music by
DUKE ELLINGTON

Cm
G
Am7
D9
G
why peo - ple tear the seam of an - y - one's dream is o - ver my head.
G♯dim
Am7
D9
G
Gmaj 7
G7
Do noth - in' till you hear from me At least con - sid - er our ro -
Cmaj7
Cm
G
Am7
D9
G
mance If you should take the word of oth-ers you've heard I have - n't a chance
G
Am7
G
Cm
E♭
E♭maj7
E♭
E♭maj7
Cm
True I've been seen with some-one new But does that

Eb Ebmaj7 Eb Eb9 Am7 D7 G E9 Gm
mean that I'm un - true When we're a - part the words in my heart re -
D A7 D7 G Gmaj7
veal how I feel a - bout you. Some kiss may cloud my mem - o - ry
G7 Cmaj7 Cm G Am7
And oth - er arms may hold a thrill But please do noth - in' till you hear it from me
D9 G 1. G Bb7 Eb9 D9 2. G C Cm G
And you nev - er will. Do noth - in' till you hear from

DON'T GET AROUND MUCH ANYMORE

Lyric by
BOB RUSSELL

Music by
DUKE ELLINGTON

A7
Am7
D7
floor
Could - n't bear it with - out you
G7
C
C
Don't Get A - round Much An - y More
Thought I'd vis - it the club
A7
Am7
D7
Got as far as the door
they'd have ask'd me a - bout you
G7
C
F
Fm
C
Don't Get A-round Much An - y More
Dar - ling I guess my mind's
3
3

C7
C7+
F
F♯dim
more at ease
but nev - er - the - less
G7
F♯dim
G7
C
why stir up mem - o - ries
Been in - vit - ed on dates
A7
Am7
D7
Might have gone but what for
Aw - f'lly dif - f'rent with - out you
G7
1. C
2. C
Don't Get A - round Much An - y More
Missed the Sat - ur - day
More.

LOVE FOR SALE

Words and Music by
COLE PORTER

Love for Sale - 3 - 1

Bbmaj9
Eb
Bb
Ab7
Db
Ebm
Bbm
F7+5
Bbm7
Ebm7
Ab7
Db6
Bb7
F7-9
D
Gb
Go7
C7
mp espress.
mf
Who would like to sample my supply?
Who's pre-pared to pay the price
For a trip to par-a-dise? Love for sale.
Let the po-ets pipe of love
In their child-ish way,
I know ev-'ry type of love
Bet-ter far than, they.
If you want the thrill of love,
I've been thru the mill of love;
Old love, new love,

B7
F07
Bb7-5
Eb
Eb6
Bbm
Bbm9
rall.
più rit.
f a tempo
Ev-'ry love but true love. Love for sale,
Eb
Eb6
Bb
Bbmaj9
Eb
Ap-pe-tiz-ing young love for sale.
If you want to
Ab7
4fr.
Db
4fr.
Ebm
6fr.
F7+5
molto cresc.
ff broadly
buy my wares, Fol-low me and climb the stairs, Love for
Bbm
Bbm7
Bbm6
Eb7
Ebm7
6fr.
F7+5
dimin.
p
sale. Love for
E07
Ebm6
Bb
Bb
dim. e morendo
pp
1.
2.
sale. sale.

I'LL NEVER SAY "NEVER AGAIN" AGAIN

Words and Music by
HARRY WOODS

F
you a - gain", 'cause here I'm kiss - ing you a - gain;
Gm7
C7
Gm
C7
C+
F
B♭
that's just the thing I said I'd nev - er do.
F
F7
Fdim
F7
I walked a - way and said "good - bye",
B♭
F+
B♭
G7
Gdim
I was has - ty, was - n't I?
I missed you so, I

G9
G7
C7
thought I'd die, — but it's all o - ver now, throw my hat in the sky! — I'll
C7
F
nev - er say "nev - er a - gain" a - gain, — 'cause here I am in
Gm7
C7
Gm
C7
love a - gain, — head o - ver heels in love a - gain — with the
G7
C7
1.
F
Gm
Adim7
2.
F
same sweet you! I'll you! —

LOVER, COME BACK TO ME!

Words by
OSCAR HAMMERSTEIN II

Music by
SIGMUND ROMBERG

F7
sus 4
F7
Gm
rall.
A7
D7
sus4
D7
met you Seems to stay for - ev - er in my mind.
mf
rall.
Refrain
G
p - f a tempo
B7
Em
The sky was blue, And high a - bove The moon was new
p - f a tempo
A7
G
A7
D7
And so was love. This eag-er heart of mine was sing - ing:
G
C
Cm6
G
D7
G
"Lov - er, where can you be?" You came at last,

B7
Em
A7
Love had its day,
That day is past,
You've gone a - way.
G
A7
D7
G
C
Cm6
This ach - ing heart of mine is
sing - ing:
"Lov - er, come back to
G
B7
Em
Am
Em
me!" When
I re - mem - ber ev - 'ry lit - tle
thing you used to do,
B7
poco accel.
F♯-9 sus4
F♯-9
B7
Em
a tempo
I'm so
lone - ly,
Ev - 'ry road I walk a - long I've
poco accel.
a tempo

Am
Em
A7
D7
sus4
D7
walked a - long with you,
No won - der I am lone - ly.
G
B7
Em
The sky is blue,
The night is cold,
The moon is new,
G♯dim
Am
rit.
a tempo
G
Am
D7
But love is old,
And, while I'm wait-ing here, This heart of mine is sing-ing:
rit.
a tempo
G
C
Cm6
1.
G
D7
2.
G
"Lov - er come back to me!"
me!"

DON'T SIT UNDER THE APPLE TREE
(With Anyone Else but Me)

Words and Music by
CHARLIE TOBIAS, LEW BROWN
and SAM H. STEPT

Chorus, Brightly
F
C7
D7
Gm7
Cm6
G7
B♭
mp
Don't Sit Under The Apple Tree with any-one else but me,
An-y-one else but me,
An-y-one else but me, No! No! No!
Just re-mem-ber that I've been true to no-bod-y else but you, So
just be true to me.

F
C7
F
D7
Don't go walk-ing down lov - ers' lane with an - y - one else but me,
Gm7
C7
Gm7
C7
F
Gm7
C7
F
C7
Gm7
C7
An - y - one else but me, An - y - one else but me, No! No! No!
F
C7
F
Cm6
D7
Don't start show-ing off all your charms in some-bod - y else'- s arms, You
G7
Gm7
C7
F
Gm7
F
F7
B♭
must be true to me. I'm so a - fraid that the
mf

Gm7 C9 F C7 F A7 Dm Dm7
plans we made un-der - neath those moon-lit skies Will fade a - way and you're
Dm6 G9 C7 Dm7 Cdim C7 C7 aug F C7
bound to stray if the stars get in your eyes, So, Don't Sit Un-der The
F F Cm6 D7 G7
Ap-ple Tree with an-y - one else but me, You're my L -
Gm7 C7 1. F Bb F Cdim Gm7 C7 2. F Bb6 F
O - V - E. E.

JERSEY BOUNCE

Words by
BUDDY FEYNE

Music by
BOBBY PLATER, TINY BRADSHAW
and EDWARD JOHNSON

G9
C
Ab9
4 fr.
C
put it right on the air ____ And now you hear it ev - 'ry - where _
C9
Bb9
Ab9
4 fr.
Up - town gave it new licks Down - town add-ed some tricks No town
G7
G7+5
C
makes it sound the same _ As where it came from! So if you don't feel so hot _
D9
G9
Go out to some Jer - sey spot. ____ And wheth - er you're hep or not _
C
Ab9
4 fr.
1
C
Ab9
G7
2
C
The JER - SEY BOUNCE-'ll make you swing. _ They ____

GET HAPPY

Words and Music by
HAROLD ARLEN and TED KOEHLER

B♭7
E♭m
6fr.
A♭m6
E♭m
6fr.
I have found a land where the wear - y for - ev - er are
C♭7
A♭m6
B♭7
free, come you sin - ners and just fol - low me
cresc.
ff
CHORUS (Lively)
E♭6
B♭7
Cm
3fr.
E♭6
B♭7
E♭
For - get your troub - les and just GET HAP - PY You bet - ter
p-f
E♭6
B♭7
Cm
3fr.
A♭
4fr.
E♭
E♭6
B♭7
Cm
3fr.
chase all your cares a - way Sing Hal - le - lu - jah, come on, GET

Eb6
Bb7
Ebm
6fr.
Eb
Bb7
Ab
4fr.
Eb
Ab
4fr.
HAP-PY Get read - y for the judge-ment day The sun is
Ab6
Eb7
Ab6
Eb7
Ab
4fr.
Ab6
Eb7
Ab6
shin - in', come on GET HAP-PY The Lord is wait-ing to take your hand
Eb7
Ab6
Eb7
Shout Hal - le - lu - jah! come on, GET HAP-PY We're go -
Ab
4fr.
Eb7
Ab6
Ab7
Db7
4fr.
ing to the prom-ised land We're head - in' 'cross the Riv - er, wash your

C7+5
F7
Bb7
Ab7
Db7
4fr.
C7
F7
sins 'way in the tide. It's all so peace - ful on the oth-er
dolce
Bb7
Eb
Eb6
Bb7
Cm
3fr.
Eb6
Bb7
Eb
side Forget your troub-les and just GET HAP-PY You bet-ter
Eb6
Bb7
Cm
3fr.
Ab
4fr.
Eb
Eb6
Bb7
Cm
3fr.
chase all your cares a - way Shout Hal-le - lu - jah! come on, GET
Eb6
Bb7
Eb
Bb7
1. Eb
B7
Bb7
Bb
2. Eb
HAP-PY Get read - y for the judge-ment day For-get your day

JUST ONE OF THOSE THINGS

Words and Music by
COLE PORTER

G♯dim F Em7 ♭5 C♯dim A7 Dm F7 B♭ G♯dim
"Don't for - get to drop a line to me, please", As Jul - iet cried
F Cm D7 Gm sus 4 Gm Dm Gm7 A7
in her Ro - meo's ear, "Ro - meo, why not face the fact, my dear?"
REFRAIN
A7 Dm A F7
p - mf
It was just one of those things, Just one
p - mf
Bm7 ♭5 C♯dim F Fm Gm7 C7
of those cra - zy flings. One of those bells that now and then rings,

Dm7
F♯dim
C7
A7
Dm
Just one of those things. It was just one of those
A
F7
Bm7 ♭5
C♯dim
F
nights, Just one of those fab-u-lous flights, A trip to the
G♯dim
F
Gm7
C7
Dm7
F♯dim
Fm7
B♭7
moon on gos-sa-mer wings, Just one of those things. If we'd
E♭
B♭7
E♭
G7
G7
thought a bit of the end of it When we start-ed paint-ing the town,

Am7
F♯dim7 ♭5
Fm7
mf
Dm7 ♭5
Em7
D
We'd have been a - ware That our love af - fair Was too hot not
cresc.
mf
F♯dim
C
p A7
Dm
A
to cool down. So good-bye, dear, and A - men,
p
F7
B♭
Gm7
Am
D7
Here's hop - ing we meet now and then, It was great fun, But it was
F♯dim
Gm
C7
F
Am
Dm
F
1.
Gm
A7
mf A7
2.
F
just one of those things. It was
mf
mf

G.I. JIVE

Words and Music by
JOHNNY MERCER

Db9 C9 F9 Db9 C9 F9 Bb9 B9 Bb Eb7
duty is to salute the L-I-E-U-T, But if you brush the L-I-E-U-T, The
Ab9 4fr. G9 Ab9 4fr. G9 Ab9 4fr. G9 G7+5 C
M. P. makes you K. P. on the Q. T. This is the G. I. JIVE, man alive, They
Optional Spoken
Dm7 G7 C C° Dm7 G7 G+ C
give you a private tank, That features a little device called fluid drive. Jack, after you revive,
C#° G7 F7 G7+5 1. C6 D7 G7+5
Chunk all your junk, Back in the trunk, Fall on your bunk. (Spoken) Clunk! This is the
2. C A7 Dm7 C#° Dm7 C#° F G7 F Bm7-5 E7+5 Bb7-5
bunk! (Spoken) Clunk! Soon you're count-in' Jeeps, But be-fore you count to five,
cresc.
A9 Dm7 C6 Fm7 F#° 4fr. Dm7 Db7+9 3fr. C Db7 4fr. C6/9
Seems you're right back digg-in' that G. I. JIVE.

I GET A KICK OUT OF YOU

Words and Music by
COLE PORTER

C7
Fm
B♭7
E♭
Gm
And I sud-den-ly turn and see _ your fab-u-lous face.
REFRAIN
Fm7
p-mf
Fm6 Fm7
I get no kick from cham - pagne, ______ Mere al - co -
hol does - n't thrill me at all, So tell me why should it be true. ______
Gm7
_ That I get a kick _ out of you? ______

Fm7 Fm6 Fm7 B♭7 E♭ Gm Fm7 Fm6 Fm7
Some get a kick from co - caine, I'm sure that
B♭7 E♭ Cm6 Gm Fm7 F7 B♭ A A♭
if I took ev - en one sniff That would bore me ter - rif - ic - 'ly
E♭ Gm Fm B♭7 E♭
too. Yet I get a kick out of you.
Gm E♭7 mf A♭ E♭7 D♭ A♭ D♭ A♭
I get a kick ev - 'ry time I see you're
Cm E♭7 Cm E♭7 Edim. C7
stand - ing there be - fore me.

Fm p Bbm6 Fm Bbm6 Fm F7
I get a kick tho' it's clear to me You ob - vious -
Fm7 Bb7 Fm7 Fm6 Fm7 Bb7
ly don't a - dore me. I get no kick in a
Eb Gm Fm7 Fm6 Fm7 Bb7 Eb
plane, Fly - ing too high with some {gal guy} in the
Gm Fm7 Bb7 C7
sky Is my i - dea of noth - ing to do. Yet
Fm7 Bb7 1. Eb Gm 2. Eb
I get a kick out of you. you.
p mf f

Recorded by BENNY GOODMAN

IT'S ONLY A PAPER MOON

Words by
BILLY ROSE and E.Y. HARBURG

Music by
HAROLD ARLEN

D7 Am7 D7 G C6 Gm7 Gmaj7 Am7 D9
believed in me. With - out your love, it's a hon - ky-tonk pa -
cantabile
G C6 Gm7 Gmaj7 G Dm E7 A9 D7+5
rade, With - out your love, it's a mel - o - dy played in a pen-ny ar - cade.
G G♯o7 Am7 D7 Am7 D9 G
p-f
It's a Bar-num and Bai - ley world, Just as phon - y as it can be,
1. 2.
Dm6 Am7 D7 Am7 D7 G Am7 D7 G
But it would - n't be make be - lieve If you be - lieved in me.
sf

IT DON'T MEAN A THING
(If It Ain't Got That Swing)

Words by
IRVING MILLS

Music by
DUKE ELLINGTON

doo wah, doo wah, doo wah, doo wah, doo wah, doo wah, doo wah,) It don't mean a thing, all you
got to do is sing, (doo wah, doo wah, doo wah, doo wah, doo wah, doo wah, doo wah, doo
wah,) It makes no diff-'rence if it's sweet or hot, Just give that rhy-thm
ev'-ry-thing you got, Oh, it don't mean a thing, if it ain't got that swing,
(doo wah, doo wah, doo wah, doo wah, doo wah, doo wah, doo wah, doo wah.) It wah.)
fz

SHORTY GEORGE

By
COUNT BASIE and ANDY GIBSON

tr
Lightly
mf
8va
8va
loco

BODY AND SOUL

Words by
EDWARD HEYMAN, ROBERT SOUR
and FRANK EYTON

Music by
JOHNNY GREEN

C
C dim
Dm7
G7
E7
me you're wrong - ing I tell you I mean it,
Am
Dm7
G7
C
Am
A♭7
I'm all for you, Bod - y and Soul!
D♭
A♭7
D♭
G♭
mp - mf
I can't be - lieve it, It's hard to con - ceive it That
D♭
A♭7
D♭
C♯m7
F♯7
you'd turn a - way ro - mance.
Are you pre - tend - ing, it

Bma7
B
C♯m7
F♯7
B7
B♭7
A7
un poco rall.
looks like the end-ing Un - less I could have one more chance to prove, dear,
un poco rall.
Dm
G7 sus C
G7
C
G7+
p - mf
My life a wreck you're mak - ing, You know I'm yours for
p - mf
C
C dim
Dm7
G7
E7
Am
Dm7
G7
just the tak-ing; I'd glad-ly sur-ren - der my-self to you, Bod-y and
1. C
A7
2. C
D♭
C
D♭
C
Soul!
Soul!
mf
mf
f

I'VE GOT A GAL IN KALAMAZOO

I've Got a Gal in Kalamazoo - 3 - 1

Eb
Fm7
Eb
Edim
Fm7
Bb7
my, how she grew; I liked her looks, when I car -
Fm7
Bb7
Eb
Eb7
Ab
Eb
ried her books in Kal - a - ma - zoo, zoo, zoo, zoo, zoo. I'm gon-na
G7-9
C7-9
Bbm6
send a wire, hop - pin' on a fly - er, leav - in' to - day.
C7
F7-9
Am I dream - in'; I can hear her scream - in', "Hy -

Eb
Bbdim
Fm7
F9
F7-5
Bb7
Coda
G7
C7
a Mis - ter Jack-son" ev - 'ry-thing's O
hur - ry-ing to.
F9
Bb7
Eb
Eb7
Ab
Abm
Bb7
I'm goin' to Mich - i - gan to see the sweet - est gal in Kal - a - ma -
Eb
Eb7
Ab
Bb7
Eb
Eb7
1.
2.
zoo.
zoo, zoo, zoo, zoo,
Ab
Eb
Ebdim
Bb7
Eb
zoo! Kal - a - ma - zoo!

IN A MELLOW TONE

By
DUKE ELLINGTON

Medium Swing Tempo (*not too fast*)

I'VE HEARD THAT SONG BEFORE

(From The Film "YOUTH ON PARADE")

Words by
SAMMY CAHN

Music by
JULE STYNE

how a theme _ re-calls a fa - vor - ite dream, A dream that brought you so close to
me. I know each word be-cause I'VE HEARD THAT SONG BE-FORE, The ly-ric
said "For - ev - er - more." For-ev - er more's a mem - o - ry.
Please have them play it a - gain, _ And I'll re - mem - ber just when I HEARD THAT LOVE-LY
SONG BE - FORE. It FORE.
rall. e dim.
f

JUMPIN' AT THE WOODSIDE

Words by
JON HENDRICKS

Music by
COUNT BASIE

G6
Jump-in'! Y' dig it com - in' thru' the door, a lot a' jump-in'! N' you can
jump-in'! Y' dig it soon as you ar-rive, a lot a' jump-in'! It's got an -
f
Am9
Am9
(D Bass)
feel the shak-in' floor, a lot of jump-in'! N' you'll be com-in' back for more.
oth - er kind of jive, a lot of jump-in'! N' real - ly ver - y much a - live.
I tell ya'
G6
1. D9
G6
2. D9
G6
jump-'n man they're jump-in' at the Wood - side now. A lot a' Wood - side now!

Voices - I gotta go - I wanna blow
I gotta go - I wanna blow.
A little room - a lotta fun
I'm goin' home - I gotta run.
Jon - Not a little mansion an' it ain't
no motel.
I'm tellin' y' where the place is,
Bet - cha - never heard o' such a
groovy hotel.
Cop a room 'n then y' really c'n
Ten' t' biz.
Voices - I gotta go - I wanna blow
I gotta go - I got a really groovy pad
the better pad I ever had.
I gotta go - I wanna blow.
I gotta go - I never ever wanna move,
I never had a better groove.
I gotta go - I wanna blow
I gotta go - a tiny room is all I rent
But, man, I really do a lot o' livin'.
Piano - Eight bars
Voices - I gotta split - I gotta go
I'm gonna blow
Annie - That's it.- That's it.- That's it.
My hotel, - really glad I live at the woodside.
It's the greatest and grooviest pad that I've ever had,
An' I lived in lots of hotels
Everywhere from Bangor, Maine all the way to L.A.
When I hit the Woodside I settled down
An' I'm there to stay,
All day - all night there's bound to be
Somebody who has a horn,
Blowin', goin' on, sure's you're born,
Swingin' from mornin' till night.
When you're feelin' tight cool it.
Fall in the sleepers,
Sleep some - rest your peepers,
Then later, when you feel greater, dig -
Jon - Jumpin' in the hall 'n everybody has a ball.
'N what a ball - I do mean,
It's jumpin' every minute.
Soon - as - y' get inside the door
Well you can feel the shakin' floor
'N that alone'll tell y' th' hotel
Is quite a jumpin' scene.
Lower the blind - get outa your mind
On women 'n wine - y' try it.
You'll dig it.
I tell y' everybody has a ball in my hotel.
What a story I can tell
Y' finish up a gig' 'n tighten up your wig.
Y' never have t' wander aroun' 'n roam
You'll never find a groovier place
T' get the jumpin' really goin' on
You can make it in 'n have a ball at home.
Dig it - you'll find - it's swell.
I dig the Woodside - man, that's where I dwell.
I tell y' really, I'm livin'
'Cause I really have a ball in my hotel.
Voices - A lot o' jumpin' - y' dig it
Soon as you arrive.
A lot o' jumpin' - it's got another kind o' jive.
A lot o' jumpin' - n' really very much alive.
A lot - o' jumpin' - I tell y' sump'n, man,
They're jumpin'.
A lot o' jumpin' - at the Woodside now.
A lot o' jumpin' - y' cop a room 'n telephone.
A lot o' jumpin' - y' tell a fella' you're alone.
A lot o' jumpin' - n' you're no longer on your own.
A lot o' jumpin' - I tell y' sump'n, man,
They're jumpin' at the Woodside now.
A lot o' jumpin' - 'n you can do the way you please.
A lot o' jumpin' - they got a place where
You can grease.
A lot o' jumpin' - 'n you can live a life of ease.
A lot o' jumpin' - I tell y' sump'n, man,
They're jumpin' at the Woodside now.
A lot o' jumpin' - y' dig it comin' thru the door.
A lot o' jumpin' - n' you can feel the shakin' floor.
A lot o' jumpin' - 'n you'll be comin' back for more.
A lot o' jumpin' - I tell y' sump'n, man,
They're jumpin' at the Woodside now.
A lot of jumpin' - y' dig it soon as you arrive.
A lot o' jumpin' - 's got another kin' o' jive.
A lot o' jumpin' - 'n really very much alive.
A lot o' jumpin' - I tell y' sump'n, man,
They're jumpin' at the Woodside now.

DAY IN - DAY OUT

Words by
JOHNNY MERCER

Music by
RUBE BLOOM

C
Dm7
G+
C
G7
Out, Day In, I need-n't tell you
Cdim.
C
Cm
Cm6
G
Dm7
how my days be - gin. When I a-wake I a-wak-en with a tin-gle,
G
Dm7
G
Bm
Am7
D7+5
one pos-si-bil-i-ty in view, That pos-si-bil-i-ty of may-be see-ing
Dm7
G7
Gm
G7
G+
C
Dm7
G+
you. Come rain, Come shine, I

C G7 Cdim. C E7+ E7+5 A7 D7+5 D7
meet you and to me the day is fine, Then I kiss your lips
Fm G+ C A7+5 D7 Dm7 G7+5
and the pound-ing be - comes the o - ceans roar, A thou-sand
C A7+5 A7 D7 Fm G7+5 C A7 C♯dim.
drums, Can't you see it's love, can there be an - y doubt, when there it
Dm7 G7 1. C Dm7-5 A♭7 Dm7 G+ 2. C Fm6 C
ten.
is, Day In, Day Out. Day Out.

SATIN DOLL

Words and Music by
JOHNNY MERCER, DUKE ELLINGTON
and BILLY STRAYHORN

Cm
3fr.
D7
Abm7
4fr.
Db7-9
C
D9
4fr.
G7-9
C
Speaks Lat-in that Sat - in Doll. She's
Gm7
C7
Gm7
C7
F
no - bod-y's fool, so I'm play - ing it cool as can be, I'll
Am7
D7
Am7
Dm7
G7
Dm7
G7
(Spoken)
give it a whirl, but I ain't for no girl catch-ing me. Swich - E- Roo-ney
Dm7
G7
Dm7
G7
Em7
A7
Em7
A7
Cm
3fr.
D7
Tel - e-phone num - bers well you know, do-ing my rhum-bas with u-no, And that 'n'
Abm7
4fr.
Db7-9
1. C
C#o
2. C
D9
4fr.
G7-9
C
my Sat - in Doll.

IT'S NICE TO GO TRAV'LING

Lyric by
SAMMY CAHN

Music by
JAMES VAN HEUSEN

G7
C6
G
C7
E
F
E
F
oh, so nice to wan-der back!
1. The mam-selles and frau - lein and the
2. You will find the maed - chen and the
Gb
G7
G9
C
G7
C
B+
B7
Em
A7+
A7
se - ño - ri - tas are sweet,
gay mu - cha - chas are rare,
But they can't com-pete, 'cause they just don't
But they can't com-pare with the sex - y
Dm
Bb9
C
Am
D9
D6
D7
Dm7
have What the mod-els have on Mad - i - son Ave.
line That pa - rades each day at Sun - set and Vine.
G7
G9-5
G9
G9+5
C6
Cmaj7
C6
Cmaj7
F7
F9
F9-5
It's ver - y nice to be foot-loose With just a tooth - brush and
It's quite the life to play gyp - sy And roam as gyp - sies will

F9 F6 F7 Dm7 G7 Dm7 G6 A♭7
comb, It's oh, so nice — to be foot-loose, But your heart starts sing - ing when you're
roam, It's quite the life — to play gyp - sy, But your heart starts sing - ing when you're
G7 Gm6 A7 A7-9 A7+ A7 Dm
home-ward wing - ing 'cross the foam. And you know your fate is
home-ward wing - ing 'cross the foam. And the Hud - son riv - er
D♯dim C Am6 B7
Where the Em - pire State is. All you con - tem - plate is The
Makes you start to quiv - er. Like the lat - est fliv - ver That
E7-9 E+ E7 Am A♭dim C7 C9 C9-5 F6 F9
view from Miss Lib - er - ty's dome. It's ver - y nice — to go
sim - ply is drip - ping with chrome. It's ver - y nice — to go

F6 Fmaj7 F6 Gm6 A7 | 1. D9-5 G7 C6 G9-5 G9 G9+5

trav-ling, But it's, oh, so — nice — to come home! 2. It's ver - y
trav-ling, But it's, oh, so — nice —

2. D9-5 G7 G9+5 C6 Dm7 G7+ C6

to come home!

3. *Special Tag Finish* (Gradual fadeout)
D9-5 G7 C9+5 C6 G Dm7 G7

to come home! No more cus - toms!

C6 G Dm7 G7 C6 G Dm7 G7

Burn the pass - port! No more pack - ing!
And un - pack - ing! Light the home - fires!
Get my slip - pers! Start a piz - za!

EXTRA HALF CHORUS

It's very chic to just drop in
On cousin Clarence in Nome;
It's very chic to just drop in,
But the thrill of all, is when you go to call
And no one's home!

The tourist ads will all tell you
That travel's cheaper than rent;
That's what the ads will all tell you,
But you'll save more dough, if you forget to go
And say you went!

COME FLY WITH ME

Lyric by
SAMMY CAHN

Music by
JAMES VAN HEUSEN

Cmaj7
C6
F9
Dm7
G7
E7
A7-9
FLY WITH ME! Let's fly! Let's fly a - way!
D9
G7
Cmaj9
C6
Cmaj9
C6
Cdim
COME FLY WITH ME! Let's float down to Pe - ru!
Dm
Dm7
G7
Cmaj7
C6
Cmaj7
In Lla - ma Land there's a
C6
C7
Fmaj9
F
B♭9
one-man band and he'll toot his flute for you, COME

Cmaj7
C6
F9
Dm7
G7
C
F7
FLY WITH ME! Let's take off in the blue!
C
Ab
Ab+
(Once I get you) Up there! Where the air is
mf
Dbmaj7
Db6
Bbm
Bbm7
Eb7
rar - i - fied, We'll just glide,
Bbm7
Eb7
Ab
star - ry - eyed. (Once I get you)

Ab+
Ab6
Db
G
Up there! I'll be hold - ing you so near,
Bbm6
Bdim
Am7
D7
Am7
D7
You may hear
G7
Bbm6
F
G7
Bb7
Dm
G7
Cmaj9
C6
An - gels cheer, 'cause we're to - geth - er. Weath-er wise, it's such
poco rall
a tempo
Cmaj9
C6
Cdim
Dm
Dm7
G7
a love - ly day! Just

Cmaj7
C6
Cmaj7
C6
C7
Fmaj9
F
say the words and we'll beat the birds down to A - ca - pul - co
Bb9
Cmaj7
C6
F9
Dm7
G7
Bay. It's per - fect for a fly - ing hon - ey -
Gm6
Bb7
A7
D9
D7
moon, they say, COME FLY WITH ME! Let's fly!
Dm7
G7
C6
C
Let's fly a - way!

SAME OLD SATURDAY NIGHT

Lyric by
SAMMY CAHN

Music by
FRANK REARDON

F
D7
1.
G9
just al - right, same old Sat - ur - day night.
where in sight,
D7
2.
Dm7
G7-9
C
C7
same old Sat - ur - day night. I real - ly thought the
F
Gm7
F
pa - pers I bought would help me for - get you for a while; Be-

D7
G9
A♭9
lieve me, hon - ey, the fun - nies were - n't fun - ny, they did - n't e - ven make me smile.
G7
C
C7
F
C
How I wish you'd lift the phone;
Am7
Dm7
G7
C
C7
fun is fun, but not a - lone;
Till you let me
F
D7
Dm7
G7-9
C
D♭7
C6
hold you tight, same old Sat - ur - day night.

FIVE MINUTES MORE

Words by
SAMMY CAHN

Music by
JULE STYNE

G7 Dm7 G7 G9 C C E+ E7
— let me stay — in your arms. — Here am I beg-ging for On-ly
p mf
F A+ A7 Dm D7 G7 Dm7 G7 G9 G7 C Dm7 C C+
FIVE MIN-UTES MORE, On-ly FIVE — MIN-UTES MORE — of your charms. —
F Fm C Cdim C C G7 Edim C7 F C E7 Am
All week long I dreamed a-bout our Sat-ur-day date. — Don't you know that Sun-day morn-ing
f
D7 G7 C E+ E7 F A+ A7 Dm D7
you can sleep late? — Give me FIVE MIN-UTES MORE, On-ly FIVE MIN-UTES MORE, Let me stay,
p mf
G7 Dm7 G7 G9 G7 1 C Dm7 Am7 E♭dim G7 2 C Dm7 C A♭7 Dm7 G9 C
— let me stay — in your arms. — Give me. —
f p f

THE SAME OLD SONG AND DANCE

*Symbols for Guitar, Diagrams for Ukulele.

Gdim G7 C7 B♭maj.7 B♭7 E♭7 C7 Cm7 F7
The same old moon - lit scene! Turns out you on - ly
B♭6 Bdim Cm7 F7 B♭6 Bdim Cm7 F7
used those eyes, Sim - ply to sell me all those lies, I real - ly went King
Fm6 G7 Bdim Cm Cm7 B7 B♭ B♭7 Cm7
Size For THE SAME OLD SONG AND DANCE! Me with the built in ra - dar,
A♭7 E♭m6 B♭
Me with the cush - ioned heart, Wind - ing up num - ber one, On the
B7 B♭ F♯9 F7(-9/+5) B♭6 B♭7 A7 A♭7
all time los - ers chart! I should for -
L.H.

G7 F Gdim G7 C7 B♭maj7 B♭7 E♭7 C7
get you, but— I won't!— Should hate you, but— I don't!—
Cm7 F7 B♭6 Bdim Cm7 F7 B♭6 Bdim
It did-n't turn out like I planned, But if you smiled and waved your hand,—
Cm7 F7 D7 G7 Cm7 F7 Fm6 G7 Bdim
I'd go and hire a band And beg for one— more chance — AT THE
Cm Cm7 1. B7 B♭6 E♭9 B♭6 B♭7 A7 A♭7
SAME OLD SONG AND DANCE! — It's just THE
2. B7 B♭6 E♭9 B♭6 F9 B♭6
SONG AND DANCE! —
8va bassa